TRUE FIT

Also by Jim Beqaj

How to Hire the Perfect Employer: Finding the Job and Career that Fit You Through a Powerful Infomercial

TRUE FIT

How to Find the Right Job by Being YOU

Jim Beqaj

Foreword by Dominic Barton
Managing Director, McKinsey & Co.

BARLOW BOOKS
fine books for enterprising authors

Library and Archives Canada Cataloguing in Publication data available upon request.

ISBN 978-1-988025-10-0 (print)
ISBN 978-1-988025-17-9 (ebook)

Printed in Canada

TO ORDER:
In Canada:
Georgetown Publications
34 Armstrong Avenue, Georgetown, ON L7G 4R9

In the U.S.A.:
Midpoint Book Sales & Distribution
27 West 20th Street, Suite 1102, New York, NY 10011

Publisher: Sarah Scott
Project manager: Zoja Popovic
Managing editor at large: Tracy Bordian
Cover design: Margie Miller
Interior design: Kyle Gell Design
Page layout: Kyle Gell Design
Copy editing: Strong Finish Editorial Design
Indexing: Wendy Thomas
Publicity: Debby de Groot

For more information, visit **www.barlowbooks.com**

BARLOW BOOKS

Barlow Book Publishing Inc.
96 Elm Avenue, Toronto, ON
Canada M4W 1P2

For my amazing wife, Jennifer,
and our six wonderful children, Emma,
Eddie, Nora, Jack, Sam, and Sarah.

For my sister Shano and her husband,
Nusret, both of whom left us far too soon.
We miss them dearly.

CONTENTS

ACKNOWLEDGMENTS

First and foremost, thank you to everyone who has trusted me to help coach them to a better place in their lives. A special thanks to those of you who kindly allowed me to present your stories and life transformations in this book. As I have said to many people, helping others find their True Fit is my calling and not a job. The joy that I feel watching people transition from confused and unworthy to confident and fully appreciative of who they are and understanding why that matters so much is incredible.

As I reflect on the publication of my second book, I know that the strong support and love from my family are at the very core of what I do. Heartfelt thanks to my amazing wife, Jennifer, who I am fortunate enough to have been married to for over twenty years and love sharing every day with, and to my six wonderful children, Emma, Eddie, Nora, Jack, Sam, and Sarah, who not only bring me great joy and pride but keep me grounded in who I am and what's really important in life—being their father.

I also want to thank my partners and friends Jaz Chahil and Bob Baldock.

Many thanks to Dominic Barton for providing the wonderful foreword to this book.

Thank you as well to the countless friends and clients who have supported me every step of the way in my own journey, allowing me into their lives to help them both professionally and personally.

Lastly, I would like to thank the team of people who have assisted me through the journey of my second book: Beth Parker, my co-writer; Sarah Scott, my dear friend and publisher; Debby de Groot, my publicist; Heather Sangster, the editor who turned my scribblings into a story; Margie Miller, the designer of this wonderful book cover; Kyle Gell, the designer and formatter of this book's interior; and last but not least, Tracy Bordian, the managing editor who kept me on the straight and narrow to get this book published on time.

FOREWORD

People are at the heart of driving performance in all organizations. In fact, in today's rapidly evolving business environment—where the average lifespan of a company is dramatically shorter than it has ever been—talent is becoming even more important as a competitive differentiator. Organizations that can both attract the right people and create conditions under which they can thrive and create value consistently outperform the competition. At the same time, we know from research by Gallup and others that the vast majority of workers are not engaged at work—a terrible waste when you consider the cost to not only individuals, but to businesses and society as a whole, from people not bringing their full energy and capabilities to their roles.

Jim's book *True Fit* makes an important contribution to our understanding of how to address these challenges. It helps both organizations and individuals understand the importance of finding the right match, providing a playbook to unleash the tremendous potential that exists when you connect the right person with the right role.

True Fit captures the personal and business imperatives of finding the best match between people and roles, and clearly outlines what it takes as an individual to identify and attain the perfect role. Jim shares compelling stories from both his career and that of others, demonstrating what good fit means for people at all stages, from new entrants into the job market to senior executives. He reinforces this with insightful analysis of the cost to companies of a bad fit, including lower morale and productivity that prevents people and organizations from reaching their potential. Moreover, he shows how creativity and innovation—essential factors for success for all companies—become impossible to deliver when people are disengaged because they are not a good fit for their roles.

As Jim suggests, finding your true fit can be a daunting prospect. Jim points out the pressures we face from various sources throughout our life to "make it work" and try to fit into whatever situation we find ourselves in. This book does a terrific job of articulating the need for self-reflection—understanding the "real you" instead of relying on others to ask the right questions or tell you about yourself. Jim also highlights the need to stop relying on traditional methods for approaching prospective employers and advocates that we focus on our strengths and arm ourselves with a CV that provides true insights into our personality, not just one that describes our experience.

Drawing on a wealth of experience hiring others as well as his own personal history finding the right fit for himself, Jim provides very practical tools for finding the right fit. His description of the core principles of networking are incisive, and applicable regardless of one's industry or stage of career. He also offers a personalized approach to how people can unlock their performance that is applicable to both those entering the workforce the first time and seasoned executives, such as putting together the right "infomercial" to share with prospective employers as you seek the right fit.

Ultimately, Jim's approach to developing your own story and "infomercial" centres around asking the right questions of ourselves, ranging from personality-based questions on how you prefer to resolve conflict and what your perfect day would look like to practical ones such as exactly what an employer should be paying you for. In addition to thinking through your personality and utilization "bandwidth"—and making sure to use these to drive research and decision making when seeking a role—Jim articulates how to use your "infomercial" to find the right set of target employers, pointing out that one should think across industries and sectors.

But the messages and tools of *True Fit* go beyond simply finding a job; they apply equally to evaluating your current position and understanding how and when to get out of a wrong fit. Jim shares compelling stories of how a variety of professionals have been able to stay true to themselves and get out of the wrong fit using the methodologies he describes. His concluding remarks on common objections to finding the right fit is equally convincing—and a terrific way to assuage the typical concerns we have when working through such a process.

True Fit captures the imperatives for individuals and organizations to find the right match of capabilities and roles—and provides an excellent guide for each of us in our quest for a true fit.

Dominic Barton
Global Managing Partner,
McKinsey & Company

INTRODUCTION: WHAT IS A TRUE FIT?

Be you. The world will adjust.

If you ask senior-ranking people in most corporations whether they hire for fit, they'll tell you, "Of course we hire for fit." "Fit" is paraded around in hiring circles like Mom's apple pie—the cure for all ills. And yet corporations are notorious for making wrong hires. There are countless stories about people who have gone to a company to do a specific job but weren't given the authority, the tools, or the air support to get anything done. They were ejected within months. No one could have succeeded under those conditions.

I know because I was one of these "bad fits." I was fired, twice. I had to figure out a different way to find work and be happy in my work because the way I was going about it wasn't yielding any success. So I looked hard at what I had learned from working inside Canada's largest, most prestigious financial institutions, where I myself had hired more than four hundred people.

Then I set up a coaching business to advise senior executives, bank presidents, and CEOs on how to recruit the best talent and to advise people looking for employment on how to prepare. My mission, for both employers and job hunters, was to achieve what I call a "true fit."

Finding a true fit requires a change in mindset. You need to change how you think about yourself so that you look at opportunities in a different way. The focus isn't "the job." It's about finding you—what you like to do best, who you like to work with, and how you can deliver value to a prospective employer. Once you define yourself, it is much easier to find the job that's right for you.

I reached this conclusion by looking at my own story. At one time, I thought I was whatever job title was posted on my office door or on my business card. I'd spent a lifetime trying to fit in, trying to please someone else. I wanted to win the prize, even if it was a prize I didn't actually want. When it came to my career, the focus was always on how to be picked, win the interview, and land the job. Then, once I got the job, I focused on how to achieve the promotion, and be the one who could bring about change even though some of those people around me wanted everything to remain the same.

After I was fired a second time, I finally took stock. All my life I had wanted to win so badly that I was prepared to change who I was. Why would I do that? Why would I want a job if it meant changing who I am? I began to formulate questions that would force me to look inside myself, acknowledge my true worth, and help me resist the temptation to be moulded into what someone else wanted me to be. These then became the questions I use to help others find a true fit.

A true fit is when you use most of your best skills every day in an environment in which your character is compatible with the character of the people around you. When there's a true fit, you know it. Your job is not routine; it's enjoyable and rewarding every day. You go home from work fulfilled, and you're glad to start work in the morning. You're more productive and creative on the job. You need less supervision. You're having fun.

Sound good? Well, it's not easy to achieve. You have to be honest about who you are, and what you're good at—or not. You have to understand your own personality—who you like to work with, and how tolerant you are of different kinds of people. The *True Fit* process frightens some people. I get that. When my good friend Rick picked up my first book, *How to Hire the Perfect Employer*, he quickly put it down. The mere idea of finding a job that fits scared him. It made him realize he needed to do some deep thinking before he looked for his next job.

Sure, it's scary to say, "This is who I am." But it's what you've got to do. Because in the end, you want someone to hire you because they understand who you are. You want them to hire you because the mental image you give them confirms that you are what they are looking for, and they want to use *all* of what you have to offer.

It's not about the job; it's about finding *you*.

Finding yourself is hard, but the consequences of not going through the process are too high. You'll end up in the wrong job, and you'll be unhappy. You'll be one of countless wrong fits, like I was years ago, when I was suddenly out on the street (again), wondering, "What happened?"

My mission is to help people avoid a wrong fit and instead find a true fit at work. My coaching business is now in its fifteenth year. Since my first book, I've gathered tangible results from people who have followed my process for finding a true fit and ended up in the right place. You'll hear from men and women of all ages, newly graduated and long-time business leaders, former politicians, board chairs, an award-winning chef, and an international beauty consultant.

In *True Fit*, each one of these clients tells their own story—and each one essentially says: Yes, it was tough; yes, I was afraid to be myself, but, yes, it works; and when it works it's empowering.

I'm not hypothesizing here. It's not that I *think* true fit is a good idea. I *know* it works. I've *seen* it work. And if you follow what others have found in this book, true fit will work for you.

chapter 1

FINDING A TRUE FIT

Either you run the day, or the day runs you.

—Jim Rohn

At thirty-seven, I was promoted into a big job on Bay Street, the financial epicentre of Toronto. I was named president and chief operating officer of a prominent investment banking firm. After leading the integration of its trading room, I wrote the strategy and executed the plan for how to grow the operations into the United States and the world by building derivatives and high-yield businesses. I relocated to New York City, and I hired more than four hundred people in eighteen months to get the operation up and running.

The integration was tough, but by most measures it was a success. And when I was finished, I wanted to keep going. I realized that this growth had put stress on the fabric of the firm, but I thought that was what I was supposed to be doing. After all, real change is never easy. The past couple of years had made good use of my skills in matching talent to the right job, coaching, and growing businesses. But I also realized that I had blown through some yellow and red lights to make it happen. My view was that we had just completed the first quarter. Now that we had these two pivotal businesses in place, we would have a launching pad to grow even faster and even bigger. Unfortunately, I wasn't aware of the stress this was causing at head office and how uncomfortable much of the old guard felt about the drastic changes I had brought in. I had lost my air support and didn't realize it.

My boss called me back to Toronto and pulled me into his office. I'd been great at what I had planned and executed, he told me, but there was a problem: "We can no longer live up to your expectations or aspirations."

"What the heck does that mean?" I asked. I soon found out. What it meant was I was out!

At first it was a relief. I was recently remarried, with another child on the way. After working in the industry for nineteen years it was a good time for a break. Still somewhat bruised, I got back on my feet. Over the next six months, I interviewed with potential employers all over the world. During this time, the CEO of a Canadian investment firm had pursued me to run its fixed income operation. I had said no several times. The job wasn't a big enough canvas for me to work on at this point in my career. In order to entice me further, the CEO laid out a smorgasbord of what I'd be able to do—build high yields and derivatives, integrate the investment and the corporate, take charge of any acquisitions. It was music to my ears. This is what I was built for. I took the job.

When the newspaper announced my new position, unfortunately none of the responsibilities the CEO had promised were mentioned—apart from running fixed income, which is exactly what I didn't want to do. On Day One, I came home and said to my wife, "I'll never be effective here."

I was depressed, my ego battered. All of a sudden I'd gone from a place where I had all the power to a place where I couldn't write a $5,000 cheque without having ten people sign off on it. I went to the CEO right away and put it bluntly: "This is not why I came here. This article doesn't reflect the deal we had." The CEO just shook his head. The reality was that he didn't care whether he was using my full capacity; he just wanted someone to run fixed income.

I knew I had made a horrible mistake, and I didn't have the intestinal fortitude to just walk away. I wanted badly to make this work, but inside I knew I was DOA. This was not the job I wanted to do, or expected to do. So instead I started interviewing on the side, slowly giving in to the slippery slope—trapped in a position where I either had to quit right away or steadily become so disengaged that I got myself fired.

I ended up with my reputation in tatters. I now had been fired twice and people assumed I was the problem.

And whose fault was that? In the end, it was mine. I had convinced myself to ignore all the warning signs—the smooth talking and nothing in writing. I refused to see the reality of the situation. My boss wanted to *talk* about change, but he didn't really understand what it took to *bring about* real change. It wasn't until I took the job that I saw the hard truth.

After my second bank job failed, I co-founded a financial start-up company. We had a wonderful idea well financed by some of the biggest names on Bay Street. Unfortunately the business was fifteen years ahead of its time to boot. Too early or too late—same graveyard.

Now, with three job losses behind me in thirty-six months, I knew there had to be a better way to find a job—a job where I could be me and be successful and happy. So I looked back on all the people I'd hired, and my own experience with the hiring process, and asked myself, "Why do we let ourselves take a job we know is not the right fit for us?" Here's why: Everyone says that they are looking for the right fit, but what they really want is a job.

Everyone says that they are looking for the right fit, but what they really want is a job.

When we're looking for a job, we'll do anything to hide our real selves so we can fit in. Then, if we land the job, we try to make it work so that we can get promoted. We settle for a job that deep down we know is not right for us, and we tell ourselves, "The right fit doesn't even exist for me."

It starts from the time we are born. Most of us get the message that we can't have everything we want in life; we have to work at the things we're not good at. We must be balanced, not tip one way or the other, and we have to get along with everybody. Parents, teachers, and guidance counsellors alike advise us to compromise, comply, bend, and, above all, "make it work."

Does that make sense? When I asked myself why the talent I had recruited in the past had been so successful, I came to a startling conclusion. It wasn't because they tried hard at things they weren't good at. It wasn't because they were necessarily balanced and got along with everybody. The key was that they did what they were really good at. And their personality fit the culture of the workplace. They were, in other words, a true fit.

Now, after a lot of stops and starts, I am the definition of a true fit. I know what I'm really good at doing. I'm really good at being a trusted adviser to my clients. I execute that role in three ways: I help them recruit, I help them figure out why businesses don't work (which usually means they have the wrong people in the business), and

I coach them and their teams to be more effective. I know I'm a true fit in my business in that I am utilizing 100 percent of the skills that I am good at, and I'm mostly not required to use any of the things that I'm not good at. At the core of my day, what I do makes for a pretty happy life. It's not perfect, though. There are always ups and downs. I wish I made more money and had more work.

People who hire me need my skills as a trusted adviser to help them recruit for a new position or to find a job that suits their abilities. But they also have to want me and the way I work. I'm like a good old-fashioned matchmaker. I work best with people who trust me to find the right fit for them. A client who's a true fit, then, needs the service I can give them and wants the way I work. They need me and they want me.

The failure to tell whether you are both needed and wanted can be a recipe for disaster, as you will see in the next chapter.

chapter 2

THE TRAGEDY OF THE WRONG FIT

Life is so damn short. For f*ck's sake just do what makes you happy.

—Bill Murray

A friend of mine is a brilliant derivatives player. He had a very successful career at a bank where they gave him total freedom to do what he wanted, hire who he wanted, and fully exercise all his ideas and plans. Then, after a change in management, he and his team were out. So he started interviewing with everybody. He was looking for a company that would give him the same freedom that had made him so successful at his previous job. Sure enough, he landed a seven-figure-a-year job. I called him the first day of his new job: "Congratulations, but you've made a big mistake. I bet you $1,000 you won't be there at the end of year one." He swore and hung up on me.

I was sure I had made the right call. I knew the executives, I knew the organization he had just joined, and I knew he would never be given the bandwidth he needed to use all his skills. I knew because I had been in the exact same situation. When we met a few months later, he admitted that my comments were prophetic. "I'm trying to make these changes and they're not letting me," he said. "When I presented a plan for business growth, I didn't even get a yes or no; it just went from committee meeting to committee meeting, and eventually just sat there."

Soon after he arrived, one of the senior guys in the company asked if he had everything he needed. "What I need," my friend responded, "is six thousand square feet. Let me hire about two hundred people and give me $1 billion in capital. Then leave me alone." "Very funny," the senior executive said. "That's never going to happen." But that is exactly what was needed for my friend to be able to maximize his skill set. Both parties had made a huge mistake: the company for hiring him and not understanding how to utilize him, and my friend for thinking that they understood what it meant to hire him.

It was a wrong fit, and unfortunately, it happens all the time. According to a 2016 study from the Hay Group, the world's top recruitment firm, half of Canadians are unhappy at work because they're stuck in a wrong fit. Wrong fit is expensive for employers. On average, the cost of termination for any employee in any organization can range from three to five times their annual salary.

But the non-monetary cost is even higher, both for employees and employers. Wrong fit sucks the energy out of the company, the employee, and everyone around that employee. Working together becomes a grind because of the constant waste of energy from trying to make something work when there's no possibility of that happening. Individuals put forth the effort to try to change themselves, but it just doesn't succeed—and the result is disengagement. People show up every day, attend their meetings, prepare their reports, complete their sales calls, but they are simply going through the motions. A recent Gallup study concluded that only 30 percent of North American employees feel engaged or inspired at their jobs and the vast majority of North American workers —70 percent—are not reaching their full potential.

Cost of Wrong Fit = Three to five times the employee's annual salary

The same study reports that widespread disinterest and unhappiness in the office is not only affecting company performance but is costing North American companies from $450 billion to $550 billion a year.

These are the studies and the numbers, but as a coach, I hear the stories directly from the source: the people who are suffering the consequences of a truly wrong fit at work. I'm constantly meeting and talking with people who are totally misaligned when it comes to what they are doing and who they are doing it for—and as a consequence they are miserable.

THE COMPANY WANTED THE GOLDEN BOY BUT NOT WHAT HE COULD DO

My friend the derivatives player, for instance, was known for his ability to build creative, financially successful businesses—that's the kind of guy he is. "I am a constructive disturber," he said. "That's what I want to do when I come to work each day in order to build a business."

He was a golden boy, and that's probably why the bank wanted him. But what they needed was a utility player, or a "business maintainer," as my friend put it. As a result, he was trapped in a company that wasn't using anywhere near his total capacity. It's a bit like a hockey player being put in net when he's a top goal scorer. Sure, he'll stop some goals, but he'll never do what he's good at doing, and before long he'll fail as a goalie.

They might need your skills—but do they want the way you work?

The cost for my friend was time. He lost almost a year in which he could have been building his own business. He described that year as frustrating, full of inner turmoil and boredom, and he felt like a fraud because he wasn't using the full capacity of his skills and he wasn't getting anything done. His reputation was at risk, and he knew it.

WHEN WINNING IS EVERYTHING—EVEN MORE IMPORTANT THAN GETTING THE RIGHT JOB

Wrong fit can happen for lots of reasons. Another example is Steve, who had many years of experience working with boards and associations. When he applied for a job, he got caught up in the idea of "winning" a job instead of asking the right questions. One job he interviewed for had more than four hundred applicants. "I figured, this must be a good position," he told me. "Look at how many people are applying for it."

Almost immediately after he started, Steve found out that it was the president and vice-president who had wanted to hire him, not the board of directors. "I didn't know that the message from the board from the very beginning was, 'If you hire this guy, we're not going to support him or you.' As a result, my first board meeting was cold as ice. No one wanted to listen to me.

"I had walked into the middle of a food fight," Steve recalled. "Those who hired me were held in contempt by the rest of the group. I felt I never had a chance. After a year and a half, it was over."

During the interview process, Steve missed what was really going on at the organization because he wasn't looking for it. He listened to what he wanted to hear and fell for the sales pitch from the president. "I was too passive," he said afterwards. "I was so caught up in wanting the job that I didn't find out that it might have been the right job for someone, but certainly not for me."

Like so many I've seen, he was trapped and, after a year and a half of frustration, put in a position where he had to walk away from the job. Then he had to explain to others why it didn't work out because typically in these situations most of the embarrassment is shifted to the candidate. "He just didn't work out," they say, or "He wasn't who we thought he was." Wrong fit also shakes the individual's confidence to the core. Steve questioned himself afterwards, wondering what was wrong with him. "I should have known," he told me.

WHAT WAS HE HIRED FOR?

Sometimes people are hired for their expert abilities, but it's a wrong fit because they're not given the authority or the resources to carry out the task.

A brilliant young man from Africa moved his family across the ocean to accept what he believed was a dream job in Canada. He settled in the suburbs, and every day he did a gruelling commute into the city to show up at a job with which he had become unhappy.

When he was hired, David believed that he would be implementing a new, progressive strategy related to data management and that the institution was aligned. What he didn't realize was that he was also expected to sell what he was trying to change. But he lacked the authority, the power, and the presence to get anyone on his side. At the same time, the organization itself hadn't agreed on where the problem was.

As a result, David had great difficulty succeeding. The stress of knowing that he wasn't in the right job started to impact his performance as well as his and his family's happiness. The work, of course, also wasn't getting done. In the end, from the company's perspective, it would be all David's fault.

But no one could have succeeded in this job. The company was facing overwhelming problems, including internal conflict and competing egos. Sure, the organization should have figured out and secured ownership from internal leaders and sought someone to deliver the overall data management strategy. But instead they hoped that by plugging someone to fix one of the symptoms, all the problems would somehow sort themselves out. And if they didn't, they'd just hire someone else.

"NOBODY TOLD ME IT WAS THIS BAD HERE"

Our next tragic "wrong fit" story is of an American financial executive hired to head up risk management at a Canadian company. Apparently, the decision to hire him was driven by the prestigious name of his former employer. All the talk at the time was that the interviewee was from a prominent Wall Street firm. What they didn't tell him during the interview process was that once he accepted the position, he'd have to fix some major internal problems. And he'd never done that kind of clean-up before.

So the man moved to Canada, leaving his family in New York, unaware of what he was stepping into. A year later, I visited him in his office and found him rocking in his chair. There were no pictures on the wall, no papers, no files, no signs of him settling in.

"Nobody told me that it was this bad here," he said. "I don't know if it's even fixable, but I'm certainly not the person who can do it. I'm unhappy, my wife is unhappy, my family is unhappy. I'm trapped!"

The man spent the next year wondering what was going to happen next, asking himself, Do I leave? Or do I wait to get pushed? He was angry that he wasn't told of the situation ahead of time. Trouble is, he didn't ask; like so many in an interview situation, he was wooed into taking the wrong job. A year and half later, he left, at a big expense. It was a disaster on both sides. He did a lot of damage to the company as well as to his own reputation, and the corporation was left with the same internal problems and had to start over again to find someone new.

The sad thing is that some people knew that the individual was the wrong fit from the beginning. He didn't have the skills or the experience the company needed. He was enticed into a job totally unsuited to his skills. And he accepted because, well, it was a very good job.

This is something I see all the time, especially in large organizations. Everyone recognizes wrong fit—except the person who's hired the candidate. The disconnect happens because that person hasn't listened to or asked those around them. The people doing the hiring don't perform the due diligence necessary to really understand what they need ahead of a hiring decision. They just go ahead. In their desperation to solve a problem, they ignore the signs that tell them that the basic skill set or experience is missing. Or they get star-struck by a name on a CV because they like the idea of saying "Here's our new vice-president. He's from the largest bank in the world, and we're so special, we convinced him to come *here!*"

"YOU'RE A BIT RESERVED"

Sometimes the problem is personality type. An organization might be a right match from a skills perspective, but the new employee's style of working might not be compatible with those around them.

At first everyone is willing to "try to make it work," but over time the mismatch becomes noticeable.

A brilliant young woman got a job working for a consulting company. She was very good at what she did and certainly had the skills required for the position, but she kept getting the same comments on her performance review. "We like your work, but you're a little too standoffish," said one reviewer. "You're a bit reserved," said another, who then added, "You don't even socialize well."

The fact is, the woman is a bit of a nerd (and proud of it). Her friends are nerdy—they always have been. These are the people she likes to be around. Those she works with, however, aren't like her. They enjoy more socializing both inside and outside the office. "When all my colleagues at my company go out to party, it's not who I am," she told me sadly. "So I'm working to change how I am." I told her, "No. What you should be working at is changing jobs!"

Individuals like this woman accept jobs even though right from the beginning they get the feeling they are out of step with everybody else. If the company seems to be full of boisterous, outgoing people, the person says, "This will be good for me," and if everyone works quietly behind closed doors, they think, I'll bring them around. But over time, they gradually feel more and more like an outlier. They continually ask, "What's wrong with me?" If they try to fit in and act differently than who they are, they feel like a fraud.

How long can you last, going to work every day and feeling like you have to change who you are to feel happy at work? You have to ask yourself the same question I asked the woman: "Why the heck would I do that?" Tell yourself instead, "Be me. The world will adjust."

Occasionally someone is able to see a wrong fit ahead of time and has the courage to speak up before things go farther off track. In early 2016, baseball fans were shocked when golden boy Alex Anthopoulos rejected an offer to stay on as the Blue Jays' general manager. After Mark Shapiro was named as the team's new president, Anthopoulos explained that staying on with the team "just didn't feel like this was the right fit for me going forward."

Wrong fit is costly, most of all to the individual. Anthopoulos had the courage to say that he couldn't stay given who he was and how he best worked. Although we may never know all the details, in order to protect his reputation and who he is, he accepted that it was his responsibility to avoid being hired for a position that was the wrong fit.

You can't depend on other people to figure out who you are. You can't trust that they will ask the right questions, tell you what's really going on inside their organization—or that they even know. At the end of the day, you are responsible for yourself and for your own career satisfaction. It's up to you to let the company know who you are, and it's up to you to ask the right questions when you're being interviewed.

You can't depend on other people to figure out who you are.

This means standing up for yourself and not being afraid to be judged when you realize that the fit is never going to be right. It means not letting yourself be moulded into someone else. Sometimes it means turning down an offer that uses only a small part of your capabilities. Above all, it means coming clean about the real you—unvarnished, naked, and painfully honest. In other words, stop fighting yourself. Just *be* yourself!

chapter 3

STOP WHAT YOU'VE BEEN DOING

You can't start the next chapter of your life if you keep re-reading the last one.

—Michael McMillan

The man sitting in my office was desperate and afraid. He had been out of work for almost a year.

"So how's it going?" I asked.

"Not good," he muttered. Then he threw his hands up in frustration. "I've done everything I'm supposed to do. I've updated my resumé, I've tried various versions of an elevator pitch, I've seen everyone, networked everywhere, given out my curriculum vitae to anyone who'll take it."

"And have you had any calls?" I asked.

"No," he replied, shaking his head. "The phone hasn't rung once."

"Sorry to tell you this," I said, "but either you have no skills that are required or no one out there has a clue about who you are."

The man looked even more desperate.

"I don't seriously think my first assumption is the case," I reassured him. "But I know what's

STOP

- relying on your CV to say who you are
- using a useless elevator pitch
- networking until you're properly prepared

been happening. You've been shoving your CV in front of everyone, but you haven't given them the answer to the eternal question: What should they pay you for? And what they don't know is this: you may be exactly who they need and what they want."

"What do I do now?" he asked.

"Just stop. Stop doing what you're doing," I said. "Stop depending on your CV to tell others who you are, stop using a useless elevator pitch, stop describing yourself with meaningless words, stop networking until you've properly armed yourself, and stop trying to be someone you're not."

Like everyone else, he'd spent his entire life thinking that this piece of paper was his bible. But was it really? I suggested he look at it and ask himself these questions: Is this really the best tool available to tell people why they should hire me? Does it say what's in it for them, and who I really am?

I've never met anyone who responded yes. So why use it for this purpose? Don't get me wrong. A CV is a convention, so you do have to use one when applying for a job. But a CV reveals only one kind of information. As my client Steve put it, "Your resumé is a history of where you have been and what jobs you have held, but it doesn't show the value you bring to a potential employer."

When you give someone your CV, you're asking them to figure you out based on what you've done in the past. You're also asking them to figure out what they should pay you for. And you're leaving it to them to figure out who you are, how you work, and what you love to do. You're saying, "I'm going to rely on you, the interviewer, to understand me based on this single formulaic document I have here."

Is this productive? No. If your CV doesn't give an accurate mental image of you, then how do you expect someone else to know if they want you in their organization?

It reminds me of a young man who was applying for an internship in the sports world. Unfortunately, his resumé included a list of his summer jobs, all related to the financial services industry. Not exactly a CV that would resonate with the interviewer. But what if that reviewer knew that this same kid had won three NFL suicide pools in a row, was captain of every sporting team he had been on since the age of eight, and knows everything there is to know about the NFL, the NHL, and NCAA basketball? Would that change the interviewer's mental image of who this person is? You bet it would. What if the interviewer knew the young man is obsessed with sports and works very well with anyone who is just as obsessed? They might want a kid like this on their team. But, no, the kid's resumé says, "I've been a bank employee, but, hey, hire me for a sports job." "Sorry," the hiring manager is going to say. "Next candidate, please."

The CV is where he has been, not who he is. Two completely different mental images. There is no way that this kid's CV was able to present a mental image of who he is and why he'd be a true fit for the sports job. It was an itinerary of various jobs he had held, but these jobs were unrelated to the things he was really good at doing, to what he enjoyed doing, and to his competitive style of working.

The same criticisms apply to the so-called elevator pitch. An elevator pitch is just a rehash of a CV. Like a resumé, it is information-based, but it does not give anyone any reason to want you. And like a CV, it contains the usual buzzwords. You know the ones I mean. I am a:

- good communicator
- team player
- professional
- people person
- problem solver
- hard worker
- highly qualified candidate
- self-starter
- collaborator
- seeker of excellence
- driven and passionate employee
- responsible person

What a load of B.S. Get rid of all of them. These buzzwords tell me nothing—in fact, some of them might cause me to pause. Maybe I'm not hiring for a team player, or your definition of team means a team you control. And don't tell me you're a problem solver. I didn't know I had a problem until you brought it up.

Here's the clincher, though. At the end of the day, am I going to pay you for any of these things? Most of that stuff covered by the buzzwords is not at the core of who you are; you've learned to say those things because you think that's what people want to hear.

For example, I had one eager job-hunting candidate meet with me, and I asked him three important questions (the first one will reappear more significantly in the next chapter):

1. What should I pay you for?
2. What's in it for me to hire you?
3. How can you make me money or save me time?

He sat there for ten minutes humming and hawing and then said, "I have it! I am a good communicator."

"Well, clearly not," I said, thinking he might need a bit more coaching. "But let's carry on."

Now let's look at networking. Most people have followed the standard advice from outplacement firms: clean up your CV, call everyone you know, and network your brains out. But it doesn't work that way. Unless you've properly prepared yourself, you risk falling into the category of hapless networkers who come into someone's office and then sit down and wait in awkward silence.

Contact: "What's going on?"

Networker: "Not much. [*long pause*] Just trying to figure out what to do next."

Contact: "And what are you thinking?"

Networker: "Not really sure … trying to work it out."

Contact: "And what exactly are you trying to work out?"

Networker: "Well, I'm looking around for opportunities."

Contact: "What kind of opportunities?"

Networker: "Pretty broadly speaking, I guess, I thought I might like to try something different. Somewhere where they can maximize my skills."

Contact: "And where might that be?"

Networker: "A place that's creative would be good ... you know, a company where they need a team player, someone who likes to collaborate."

Contact: "So what would you like from me?"

Networker: "Well, if you hear of anything, I guess. Have you heard of anything?"

And so goes the conversation. The contact has no clue as to what might make a good referral, no basis on which to keep their eyes open, no sense of who the networker is. The words being spoken are clichés. They mean nothing. It's all just air.

People network because they think that just by splashing themselves all over the place someone will help them or recommend them. But the truth is, this makes someone come across as being unfocused and vague. Soon everyone is tired of hearing that they are out of work. The networker becomes like a house that's been on the market too long—or, worse, a train wreck—and the contacts just want to look away.

The reality is, if anyone knows you well enough to know what job you'd be good for, that person would have already been in touch if they had come across such a job. Stop networking until you know who you are and you're properly prepared.

Here's another bit of standard advice that I think is all wrong. I bet someone—your parents, your teachers, or maybe your boss—has advised you to work on your weakness. You're not very good at numbers? Well, roll up your sleeves and learn how to create an accurate profit and loss (P&L) statement. Not much of a salesperson? Grin and shake that hand. To me, it makes no sense. People should stop doing stuff they're not good at. They'll never be all that great at the task, even if they try really hard. Why should you work on your weaknesses instead of playing off your real strengths?

This is when I tell clients about one of our sons. At five years of age, he had brain surgery. As traumatic as that was, facing the future was more daunting. At a meeting with the educators at his school and his doctors, they made it clear to us that he would be good at doing certain things and continue to do these well and that with other things he might improve over time. But there would be things he would probably never be able to do.

The educators then presented their advice: "We're not going to spend any time on the things he's good at," they pronounced, clipboards in hand, "because he's already able to do these things well. Instead, we'll work on the activities where he might improve, and even those areas where there's little expectation."

My wife and I said, "No way. Our son is going to spend *all* his time on what he is good at, and we are going to make him outstanding at those things. Conversely, we're not going to spend any time on the things that he's not good at. This way he will enjoy his learning and build confidence for improving on what he enjoys and is good at, which will help him in everything else too."

Today, our son is entering his second year at Lynn University in the United States and killing it. Throughout his life, this amazing young man has continually scored off the charts in all the psychometric tests. He has phenomenal memory and presentation skills, and he successfully founded and helped run a business with his brother by the time he'd finished high school. He's also happy, confident, and ready for the next phase of his life. We didn't let the traditional education approach force him to learn in a standard way. We adapted his learning method to his strengths.

The same approach should be applied to what each of us does during the work day. We have to get rid of the mentality that "I have to be good at everything" or "I have to be working on the things I'm not very good at." If we don't change the way we think, we end up taking a job we figure we "ought" to be able to do, or we promise a prospective employer that we will overcome a weakness or become better at doing the task we think we need to be able to do in order to land the job.

Are you really going to be happy doing activities you aren't good at and that, therefore, you don't enjoy? What if you took all the time you spent trying to learn a piece of software, or bookkeeping, or making speeches and put it toward improving what you're already good at? You know what happens next if you don't. You inevitably screw up. Then you end up feeling inadequate, failing, being reprimanded, perhaps getting fired.

Albert Einstein is known for many things—including being the author of one of my favourite quotations: "Everybody is a genius. But if you judge a fish by its ability to climb a tree, it will live its whole life believing that it is stupid." A lot of us can end up feeling like that fish a lot of the time. It's because we're trying to climb a tree when that's what we're not really very good at.

"Take your inspiration from our son," I say to my clients. "Play to your strengths. Keep improving what you are already good at doing. Stop trying to be someone you're not." Ralph Waldo Emerson put it this way: "To be yourself in a world that is constantly trying to make you something else is the greatest accomplishment."

Here's the way I put it. I used to think there were just two truths in life—death and taxes. Now I know that there are two additional truths: what you're good at, you'll always be good at; and what you suck at, you'll always suck at.

THE FOUR TRUTHS OF LIFE:

- You will pay taxes.
- You will die one day.
- What you're good at, you'll always be good at.
- What you suck at, you'll always suck at.

chapter 4

WHAT SHOULD I PAY YOU FOR?

The only way to do great work is to love what you do. If you haven't found it yet, keep looking. Don't settle. As with all matters of the heart, you'll know when you find it.

—Steve Jobs

John had a long and successful career as a financial planner and then as a politician. He was a cabinet minister until 2011, when he lost his seat in a tight election. After being rejected by the voters, he had to figure out what to do.

John realized that the first hurdle was to come to terms with the loss. "No one wants to date someone who isn't over his or her 'ex,'" he joked. "I had to first 'get over the girl.'" He also took some time off to figure out what he wanted to do next. "I knew what I had to do to be successful in business," he said. "I knew what I had to do to be successful in politics. Now all of a sudden, I was on my own."

Job offers came in, but none of them felt right. "People would come to me and say I'm a fit for their agenda," he said. But it was their agenda, not his. "I remember telling my wife, I can do this as long as I turn myself into a pretzel that someone else wanted. But I'm not going to be successful and happy unless I'm doing something I enjoy doing."

Like most of my clients, John had to answer the universal question of life: "What should someone pay me for today?" What was his real value proposition to an employer or client? It would not be easy to answer that question, especially for a former politician.

The best way I know to figure out your true value proposition is to create what I call an infomercial. You might have seen them on the shopping channel—the infomercials hawking the wonder wallet, the fake jewellery, and the magic mop. Infomercials are corny and tacky, to be sure, but the great thing about the modern infomercial is that it explains the direct relationship between my dollar and what I get when I buy the item. It says exactly what is for sale. You either need it or you don't. If you need it, you'll likely buy it. If you don't need it, you'll pass.

The universal question of life: "What should someone pay me for today?"

The infomercial for job hunters should elicit the same reaction. You say exactly who you are, what you're good at, and why potential employers should pay you today for what you can do. The person on the other side of the table may say, "Yes, this is what I need." But if he or she doesn't, that's fine too: you've just saved yourself from taking the wrong job.

To write the infomercial, you have to answer four core questions:

1. What should you pay me for?
2. Who do I work best with?
3. How do I like to resolve conflict?
4. What's my perfect day?

The ideal format for an infomercial is four sections, each answering a specific question using five or six clear, concise bullet points. I've provided an example on page 136. Using PowerPoint to create an infomercial is ideal because it forces people to be brief.

So let's go through the questions.

WHAT SHOULD YOU PAY ME FOR?

I've taken out my wallet and you're looking at a wad of fresh fifty-dollar bills. Interested? Now complete the sentence:

Hire me because I'm really good at __________.

Ask others for their input. Think about the best things anyone has ever said about you (and the worst). Above all, be honest with yourself. And don't use any of those buzzwords listed in the previous chapter. Once you've listed several points, come up with an example or some anecdotes or accomplishments to back up the points. Note that the process is going to take a lot of work if you are to get down to the essential three activities that define why someone should hire you.

My own list has three points. The first is: "I'm really good at hiring people who are the right fit." As I mentioned earlier, I've hired more than four hundred people in my career, and I've never used a recruiter. In all but one instance, the fits were successful. And that's the example I give. My next point is: "I'm good at figuring out what's wrong with businesses by looking at the leadership running the business and how well they fit that organization." Then I tell some anecdotes of businesses I've turned around. My last point is: "I'm good at coaching and mentoring people because I have an ability for getting inside their wheelhouse in order to get them to understand who they are." As an example, I list some of the people I've coached, and I also offer to provide references and testimonials from these people.

WHO DO I WORK BEST WITH?

Look back over your life and make a list of all the people you liked working with and write down why. What kind of boss or what kind of clients did you enjoy? Did they have similar characteristics? Are they strong, loyal types? Micromanagers? Big-picture thinkers? How do they behave on a daily basis? Are they loud and boisterous, reserved, or nerdy? How do they make decisions? Do they have your back?

Still thinking about those best relationships, ask yourself, Where do you find them? Are the people you work with every day the type you can't wait to see again? Give examples of groups as well as individuals in which the outcome proved that you were working with the right people for you. What was achieved in these examples?

A former trainer of mine was training ten clients a day. So I asked her, "Who do you enjoy most?"

She replied, "I work best with everyone...." She hesitated. "Well, most everyone."

I tried again. "Exactly how many do you like to work with? You know, the ones who are great to see, make you feel good about what you're doing."

"About six," she replied. "The other four are just pure drudgery."

"Really? That's four hours that you're dreading each day! Why do you put up with that?"

"Well," she replied, "it's money. I make $125 an hour training them."

So I suggested that, given she has her loyal clients (like me) who adore her, she find four new clients who would be a better fit for her. Within the next few days, she had four new clients (and had fired the others).

My trainer put up with this situation as long as she did because she didn't think she was worthy enough to make that decision—not worthy enough to fire a client! But that single step changed everything for her. She identified what was working with the clients she loved, and why, and then set out to find more clients like them. As a result, her business has grown, she enjoys every hour of the day, and she knows exactly how to keep it that way.

When you are working with people you don't like, or who don't understand you, you constantly feel like the odd one out, like you're doing something wrong. But it's not up to you to change! I told someone the other day that she has too much horsepower for the job I was interviewing her for. Her immediate response: "I can tone it down." My retort: "Why tone it down? You're not the problem; it's the lack of fit that's the problem. Why would you try to not be you?"

And if you're spending time with colleagues or clients who you don't work best with (or don't even like), you end up not liking what you're doing. For most of us, the result will be reflected in our business success because it affects our confidence and our credibility. After a while, as one senior fellow at the University of Toronto who studies and teaches leadership told me, "You'll be seen as less than genuine."

It's great to see people record who they actually like working with. Here's how a recently graduated MBA answered the question "Who do I work best with?" in her "infomercial."

- Teams of collaborative people—people who seek the right answer
- People who are highly organized
- People who give me a good amount of autonomy
- People who are willing to provide me with regular feedback
- People who I can learn from

Then she gave an example. "Last year I was assigned to a 'dream project,' where each of us had a particular area of expertise. I was the communications person, who had to decipher the reports and write all the final documentation. Although we worked alone on specific tasks, we solved problems together where we had identified gaps and challenges along the way. I learned a lot about other areas of the business, and I loved the way we all gave each other honest feedback along the way."

HOW DO I LIKE TO RESOLVE CONFLICT?

Everyone has a predominant conflict-resolution style. However, it's not about how you resolve conflict but about whether the way you resolve conflict is compatible with the conflict-resolution style of your potential employer. Your conflict-resolution style could be, for example, competitive. If you're in an environment where avoidance and accommodation is the order of the day, you could be seen as a bully, not a team player. But if you're in a place where they're all competitive, you'll be getting high-fives all around.

I talked with a young woman, Zoe, who was very clear about her competitive nature and her desire to give—and receive—brutal honesty in order to get the best results. This is someone who works best—and is most productive—when she is put on a team of carnivores similar to her in nature. But it means that she has to ask the right questions and be clear with team members about how she solves conflict when she puts together such a team. Otherwise, the team members will split apart the first time she criticizes their work.

Zoe had to accept that her style of conflict resolution is part of who she is. She had to own it but at the same time understand that by doing nothing other than being her, others are going to perceive her in a certain light. She may think she is working collaboratively in order to get the best result, but when she's on a team of compromisers, she comes across as competitive, as win/lose. The others, if their style is accommodation or avoidance, see her as running all over them—a bully, even overbearing.

But in a competitive environment, Zoe gets as good as she gives—it's what she wants and expects. Like her, the others on the team also see the situation as win/lose, and the terms of engagement are totally acceptable.

Imagine going to work for someone where the conflict-resolution mode is competitive win/lose and you're the compromising type. From the very beginning you're going to come across as an ineffectual mouse. Your effectiveness is extremely diminished and so is your happiness. You'll feel completely out of sync before you actually get to do the job you were hired to do.

This was an issue in my own career. I consider myself collaborative. I'm determined to seek the right answer with other people. But most people aren't interested in seeking the right answer unless they benefit from it. As a result, I made others uncomfortable. I even came across as threatening. It was frustrating for me. Despite the fact that I made hundreds of millions of dollars for the companies I worked for, the perception that I was overly competitive made it impossible for me to be appreciated for my successes.

WHAT'S MY PERFECT DAY?

Describe a day or a specific project you worked on in which you were so totally absorbed in what you were doing that it didn't even feel like work.

It's not about how much money you're making, but rather what you're doing regardless of what you're being paid. Where are you, and what are you doing? Are you with others or alone? Who are you talking with? What kinds of activities are you engaged in? Think about one of those days when you came home and said, "I could do this the rest of my life."

I advised a young friend to think about her perfect day. "Don't hold back," I said, "even if it sounds like a total fantasy. Define it in as much detail as you can." She didn't need further encouragement. "My perfect day would be skiing from morning to when the slopes close," she answered. "If I could ski every day of the year, I'd be happy."

Her "perfect day" scenario turned out not to be a fantasy. By putting skiing at the centre of every day, she was then able to step back and ask, "How can I make this happen?" A whole new perspective came into view because suddenly she realized that there are industries related to skiing: ski manufacturers, resorts, trips, event coordinators, incentive companies, ski guides.... There were dozens of places where she could focus her attention on getting a job that aligned with her perfect day.

When I ask friends and clients to describe their perfect day, I often find there's a deep divide between their perfect day and the days they're actually living on the job. One beautiful day in May, I was out on the golf course with a long-time friend. As we approached the fifth hole, I popped the question. "Tom, what's your perfect day?" "Out seeing clients seven days a week," he said. "Clients, clients, clients." This man had a big job in the United States, and he was stuck in his office most days dealing with administration and regulatory issues. How did this happen to someone who is a great client guy? He was a long way from his perfect day.

Defining your perfect day helps you to drill down farther into what you are really good at doing—which is also what you are happiest doing.

One woman, Elizabeth, whom we'll hear more about later, was selling hedge funds when she realized that her perfect day was reading and talking about fashion; pursuing design and artistic activities; and learning about health, beauty, and nutrition. When she realized she could take these strengths and make them into a business, she left financial services, eventually becoming the CEO of her own beauty PR company.

This "perfect day" question can be extraordinarily revealing. John, the former politician, found

WHAT DO YOU DO ON:

a. your perfect day?

b. Monday?

Do they match?

that he really liked fixing problems, but once he was done, he wanted to move on to the next challenge. He realized he didn't want to sit in an office and deal with the same problems day after day. It soon became clear where he'd find his true fit. He founded his own business as a tax planning consultant and now sits on four corporate boards. "Today, I'm doing exactly what I'm good at and what I enjoy," he said. "And after politics, I have a family life again."

Compare your perfect day with what are you doing today. Is there a match?

So these are the four questions. Writing your infomercial can be tough. In fact, fewer than one in a hundred of my clients can easily describe their perfect day to me. Think of it as a constant refinement, getting down to simple terms and sentences that connect you with the person in front of you.

If you're having trouble, try the reverse approach: What are you *not* good at doing?

- What is the *opposite* of your perfect day? (Think about all those bad days and what made them so bad for you.)
- What kinds of people can you *not* tolerate?

For example, I'm not good at keeping quiet when I see there is a problem. This tells me that I'm not the kind of guy suited to being a member of a typical board of directors. I've found that most boards look for two things: members with pedigree or members who generally go along with what the CEO wants. I don't have that kind of pedigree, and, as I said already, I don't stay quiet when I see a problem. So I know that I'm not going to be happy on a board (and the board isn't going to be happy with me either).

I also ask people to tell me the best and worst thing anybody has ever said about them professionally so that I can get a book-end perspective of what people think of them. (By the way, I don't actually care if what people say about my client is true because it's all about how my client is perceived by others.)

Remember, the process isn't about changing who you are. It's about understanding who you are so you can be yourself and thrive. You just have to find the right environment in which that can happen.

Infomercials are like mining: we start with big rocks and constantly refine until we end up with some gold dust.

Presenting your infomercial is the final challenge.

People have lots of reasons not to use the infomercial. "I can't say that," they'll say. Or "If I say that, I'm going to sound like I'm blowing my own horn."

"Mo," I reply. "Is anyone *else* blowing your horn?"

Most of us believe that talking about ourselves is bragging. Fundamentally, it's probably because of the way we've been raised (women even more so than men). Culturally, intellectually, physically, it feels uncomfortable. But the whole concept at the core of doing such an "infomercial" is to be true to yourself. When you honestly describe who you are, you are not boosting yourself—you are actually just telling the truth. You are simply making it clear who you are. It won't feel like bragging. It will feel natural, comfortable. And now you'll be able to hold on to it and say, "This is what I'm looking for, and I'm not going to settle until I find it."

One of my clients resisted for so long that I told her I would stop coaching her if she didn't use her infomercial. Her name was Jane. We first met at a hedge funds conference, where I was part of the speakers panel. When I first explained how she needed to present herself with an infomercial, she told me I was crazy. But she was unemployed, so what started as a ten-minute conversation over coffee that day turned into several meetings where we worked together to develop her infomercial.

Jane was a pretty confident woman, with almost a decade of experience working on the trading floor and excellent skills in developing client relationships. But she'd always found herself in roles where she felt she was forced to adjust who she was in order to fit in. So we started with her perfect day. Almost immediately, she found that it helped her get rid of the clutter in her head.

Jane's perfect day:

- Being part of a team but remaining independent enough to focus on growing my own "little business" ... my client book
- Spending time reading the news, organizing my day, figuring out client messaging
- Spending time with clients, lunches/coffees
- Pitching business
- Closing a deal

Defining her perfect day helped her to finally focus on what mattered to her, what she wanted to do, and how best to present herself. Then she worked through the rest of the questions, listing what she did best and those she worked best with and defining her conflict-resolution style. Once she had completed all the steps, she felt ready to pitch herself in a very concise manner the next time there was an opportunity.

It wasn't long before she had an opportunity to interview for a job as the new managing director at a financial institution. She called me up. Although Jane wasn't sure the position was right for her, she decided that in a tough job market she should at least go through the process.

Jane would typically go into the room, let those around the hiring table spew, then ask a few questions and walk away. She said that she would usually gauge what those doing the hiring wanted her to say, and then give them what they wanted even if it didn't sound like her. "After all," she said, "it's a job."

I told her to forget that crap. "You'll just end up unemployed in a couple of years and have to start all over again."

I explained a different approach. I asked her to think about the fact that she was there to interview the employer as well be interviewed by them. Instead of showing up for the meeting and waiting for the others in the room to say something, I told her, take charge of the meeting. First, thank those in the room and note that they already have your CV. But then say, "I thought before we begin it would be helpful if I gave you an idea of who I am and what you should pay me for." I advised to have her infomercial ready but to not hand it out until she had finished presenting.

Jane agreed, even though she still felt a bit uncomfortable about presenting herself in this way. On the morning of the interview, she went into a public bathroom to practise a few times in front of the mirror. She figured if anyone walked in, they'd think she was a crazy person, but she didn't care. She went through her notes several times.

The interview began and Jane took control. She suggested to the three people around the table that she first tell them a bit about herself, what she was looking for, and that then both parties could consider if it would be a good fit. After presenting her infomercial, Jane paused. She could tell by the looks on their faces that she was not what they needed or wanted.

"That's when I knew that there was no chance that they were going to hire me," she said. Within a couple of days she received an email that read "You're not the person we're looking for."

The outcome suited Jane. When I asked, "Did you get the job?" Jane replied, "No! And I'm so happy. I never felt so empowered in my life!"

Not long afterwards, she learned from friends that the company was looking for someone they could mould. "That job was definitely not a fit for me," she said, laughing.

A few months later, Jane applied for another job. "Again, my infomercial gave me a chance to present my true character," she said. "It gave me that foundational confidence to stick with my story." This time the experience was completely different. Both sides felt like it was a good fit, and what started out as an interview turned into more of a discussion. But it was during the final phase when Jane knew for sure it was going to work. One of the senior people on the hiring team sat down with her for a final conversation. "If you don't mind me saying so, it seems to me that you're a no-bullshit kind of girl, who's tenacious and hungry for business."

"I felt so validated," said Jane. "That was exactly how I had presented myself in my infomercial. I knew right then and there that regardless of the role, my new boss knew my character and liked my character. I understand why most people innately want to fit in. But you should fit in where it is right, not by adjusting who you are to make it work."

Jane's infomercial helped her identify a company needing her considerable abilities and wanting her as a person, for who she really is. "I had to learn to forget about doing interviews the way I used to," she said afterwards. "Otherwise I'd end up right back where I started.... After I developed my infomercial, I realized, Hey, I'm applying for jobs I know I can do. The role itself doesn't matter. I want to make sure the fit is right. So I stuck with my story, stopped responding the way I thought they wanted me to, and I'm thrilled with the way things have turned out."

When Elizabeth, whom I mentioned earlier, first came to me, she was bored at work. She felt she wasn't making enough money and she had that nagging feeling that she didn't fit in. Over the previous twenty years, Elizabeth had worked in real estate and then in the financial sector with hedge funds because she was able to get people excited about what she was selling. But what she was selling held no interest for her. She felt like she was in a quagmire.

I gave her the four questions to answer.

"Doing my infomercial," she says, "was like putting my life on a whiteboard. I put myself at the centre and looked at how I could take my strengths and make them into a business. Those things I was interested in doing, and enjoyed doing, had always been there; I just needed to see them written in front of me."

As mentioned, Elizabeth realized that what she really loved was fashion, design, and working with women to take care of their beauty needs. As she slowly defined and refined who she was, she finally reached a point where she could say, "That's who I am." In fact, what she discovered is that she had the same strengths and interests she'd had since she was a young girl. The clarity and confidence she felt meant a total change in careers for her—from financial services to fashion and beauty.

Today, Elizabeth is passionate about what she does every day. She's also making more money.

"It's 100 percent better than anything I did before—money *and* happiness," she said. "The risk I took turned out really, really well."

An added benefit of the infomercial is how others can now use it. Elizabeth's infomercial, for example, gave others a clear idea of who she was. She soon received a phone call from a former associate in the financial services industry who introduced her to a leader in the emerging natural skin care industry focused on luxury brands. Today, as CEO of her own company, Elizabeth represents a dozen such luxury brands across North America.

The more people there are out there who are clear about what you have to offer, the more work you'll get. Not only can you use your infomercial in your own job search, but you can also give it to others to be your advertising department.

Just imagine what happens. Like Elizabeth, someone calls you up and says, "I have something for you that I know is a perfect fit; they need you and want you, and you will like this person."

When the infomercial is really clear, it is a powerful way to say exactly who you are.

Jamie, for instance, was vying for a job at a large institution. In the interview, he was asked right away to bring out his CV. "No," he said. "I've got something better. Let me tell you about myself." He then pulled out his infomercial and started to talk.

The interviewer was blown away. "That is just awesome," he said. "I'm going to talk to my partner right away."

Jamie knew that being hired at larger organizations involved a decision-making process with more than one interview and more than just one or two individuals. There might have been ten people in the room doing the interview, and this might have been just one stage in the process. As notes were compared and the shortlist got shorter, Jamie wanted to make sure that when someone asked, "Remind me again about that last candidate," everyone would be able to repeat exactly what he had said in his infomercial.

In Jamie's case, everyone came away with the exact same picture of who he was and what he was good at. They even remembered the same example that Jamie used to show how he'd utilized his skills. When Jamie progressed to the next interview stage, his message remained consistent across the board. His infomercial made him come across as credible, honest, and not just trying to please everyone. Then when the final decision was made, everyone could say yes or no based on the consistent image he had provided them.

This is a key point: After you've presented your infomercial—for an interview, an informal meeting, or a discussion with a new client—ask the question: "Do you have a clear understanding of who I am, or how we could do business together, or why you should pay me?" If they say yes, then great, you know that they want and need what you are presenting. If they say, "No, I don't want you" or "No, I don't have anything for you," then good. At least they know who they are saying no to.

An infomercial, then, is an incredibly powerful way to present a clear image of who you are and what value you can offer to an organization. Think of it the way I do: I want to have either a positive impact with my infomercial or a clear rejection so there's no ambiguity over whether they need me and/or want me. Or like motivational speaker

Paul F. Davis has said, "Don't stay where you are tolerated. Go where you are celebrated."

The sooner you understand yourself, stand up for who you are, and have your message resonate with the right people, the sooner you'll see opportunities differently and recognize the difference between a true fit and a wrong fit. It empowers you; it fills you with confidence.

chapter 5

FINDING A JOB THAT FITS YOU

If you can do what you do best and be happy, you're further along in life than most people.

—Leonardo DiCaprio

It's always up to you, the candidate, to figure out if a job is right for you. If you create your infomercial, it gives you the clarity to ask questions and state clearly what you would bring to the company and what your style of working and resolving conflict would be. Then it should be clear to both you and your prospective employer whether it's a true fit.

The infomercial is a crucial way to define yourself and your value to a future employer. But how do you find the targets—the people who are potentially your true fit employers?

YOUR TARGET-RICH ENVIRONMENT

Let's start with your target-rich environment. It's where you should be looking for a job, given everything—your skills, experience, character, working style, and personality—you have to offer.

All our lives, people say give me your CV, tell me where you worked before—because it's all

When you look for a job or a business opportunity, you have to consider three key concepts in addition to the four core questions discussed in the last chapter:

- Your target-rich environment—Where should you be looking for a job or opportunity?
- Your personality bandwidth—Who can you deal with?
- Your capacity utilization—How much of you do they want?

about "the job." But the concept that one's skills are only applicable to a particular type of job, in a single industry or sector, is ridiculous. Once you've written your infomercial, you can find great opportunities in a lot of different places. A computer programmer who likes to sell doesn't have to resign himself to days at the office looking at a screen. His target-rich environment could include sales, consumer testing, even teaching at a college.

You need to do your homework to figure out your target-rich environment. This takes some research online and talking with others to make sure. Keep asking yourself, "Am I looking in the right places?" Look again at the list you made of who you work best with. Where do people like that work? Is it in a quiet office or a rambunctious, wide-open space—or in a country house? What would work for you? That's your target-rich environment.

One of our family's young friends, a woman in her twenties, is an excellent teacher, but she loves to do so much more than just teach. She enjoys outdoor education and travelling. She's particularly good at adapting to new situations. So when she applied for teaching positions at several traditional private schools in the city, I asked her, "Does this *really* match what you love to do?"

She was surprised at the question, and it got her thinking. Like many of us, she thought narrowly when she talked about employment; she equated a title or profession with a specific job. Since graduation, she had seen herself as teacher confined to a classroom. But as a person, she was so much more than just a title like "teacher."

It wasn't until she identified those things she loved to do—her perfect day, the people she liked to work with—that she was able to see a much wider choice, going beyond a specific industry.

She ended up in a job teaching overseas instead of stuck in a formal classroom in Toronto. It wasn't a "job"—it was a place where she could be most successful given her skills and who she is. It was a true fit for an adaptable young woman looking for adventure and new experiences.

It took my good friend Rick almost thirty years to realize that his target-rich environment was bigger than he thought. During high school, Rick played drums with a bunch of guys who ended up becoming the well-known rock band The Tragically Hip. Rick put his drums aside, pursued mining engineering, completed a master's degree, and then worked in international mining companies. Even though he had landed in an industry that appeared to be the right fit for his qualifications, it didn't feel right. "All those years, it was always about the job," Rick told me. "It was never about who I am or about finding a place where I'd really fit in."

Rick left mining and came to me. He was being recruited by Canadian banks, and he didn't want to make the same mistake as before. Rick was finally ready to figure out where to find a true fit. It wasn't easy; in fact, you'll remember that he was the one who told me that the idea of finding the right fit initially scared him.

"My God, I thought as I started to answer the four questions," he recalled. "I should have continued to play drums in a rock and roll band.... It honestly freaked me out a bit."

After his infomercial was complete, Rick knew that he needed to find a fit where he could more fully use his strengths in dealing with people and developing relationships. He made the choice to accept a job in investment banking. "I used to think I was a miner who happens to do investment banking; now I know I'm an investment banker who likes mining but is much happier at the relationship side of things. I love dealing with the clients and helping them out," said Rick. "I'm telling you, I have never been happier in my life or more at peace with myself."

Rick's narrow view of who he was restricted his choices of where to look for job opportunities. It meant that he had ended up working as an engineer in the mining industry because that was his "title." He admitted that he kept learning in his job to add value so he could get the next mining job. After Rick developed his infomercial, he finally understood his target-rich environment—which for him extended beyond mining. And now, working with people who understand him, Rick is happy and finally feels, after thirty years, that he fits in.

YOUR PERSONALITY BANDWIDTH

Before you start looking for work, it's important that you understand your personality bandwidth. Personality bandwidth is a little different from the "Who do you like to work with?" question we explored in the previous chapter. It measures your tolerance of different personalities. The range of personalities you can work with helps determine your personality bandwidth. If someone gets along with everyone and everyone loves them back, then they have a wide personality bandwidth. If someone is only comfortable with certain kinds of personalities, and only certain kinds of people are comfortable with them, then they have a narrow personality bandwidth.

I was interviewing an individual for a marketing job in Canada. He was anxious to get the job and told me all the reasons he would be suited to the role based on his CV and past experience. So I asked him, "What's the worst thing anyone has ever said about you?" He replied without hesitation, "I don't suffer fools very well. Most people piss me off."

The candidate's answer told me that he might have a very narrow personality bandwidth—and therefore be entirely unsuited for this particular job. Like others with a narrow personality bandwidth, he had strong sense of the personalities he wanted to be around and those he wanted to avoid. This gave him an approach that could rub others the wrong way. It's okay for him to be bespoken in this way, but he needed to understand how narrow his world was. He would work best in a place where his work spoke for itself and he didn't have to interact a lot with people. As a marketer for products, he would have to work with every level in the organization; in this kind of sales-generation role, he'd be a disaster.

A broad personality bandwidth, on the other hand, is like being able to speak numerous languages. Typically, people with a broad bandwidth have jobs in customer service, client relationships, and sales. They don't care if someone is difficult or overbearing because by their very nature—their personality bandwidth—they get along with everyone. They can communicate with a wider variety of personalities; clients and friends are one and the same. They find it easy to be empathetic and can almost instantly connect on some level with everyone.

Those with broad personality bandwidths can tolerate a diverse range of personality types, and they see the best in all they meet. Those with narrow bandwidths have to choose their clients or employer more carefully. For that marketing job, I knew the company needed someone who loves everyone because that's what makes for a great salesperson, not someone who finds most personalities difficult to deal with.

You have to know and accept how you are because your bandwidth isn't going to change. And those around you will see and judge you by it. I have a narrow personality bandwidth. My friends tell me I'm best served unvarnished. I don't get along with everyone; many find me brash, and I can make people uncomfortable. I have to be confident enough to say that's who I am—not in a rude way, but this is who I am. If you hire me, you are going to get the unvarnished version. If you want someone to flatter you, hold your hand, then I'm the wrong person. But if you want a trusted adviser, someone who can't help but tell you the truth, who's really good at coaching and mentoring, then I'm the one.

If you don't understand your own personality bandwidth, you may feel like you're pushing a string most of the time. Some people can live with this; others have to do something about it.

YOUR CAPACITY UTILIZATION

Finally, it's crucial to assess whether a potential employer wants all of your capabilities or just some of them. How do you do this? Depend on your infomercial to measure how close an opportunity comes to being a true fit. Use it to assess your current employment situation. Use it to identify an opportunity that's worth pursuing further, a referral that's right for you, or an industry sector you've never considered before. And use it to spot the red flags. Say no if you have to—and feel good about that decision.

Capacity utilization tells us whether the job you're considering accepting is going to utilize all of your capacity or just a little of it. Consider the five-thousand-yard passing quarterback. He's an excellent quarterback, but, ideally, he wants to be on a team that throws the ball 100 percent of the time. So what happens when he's recruited to a team that wants him to execute a playbook that has the team running the ball? It's a recipe for disaster. The coach isn't going to be interested in his passing ability because he doesn't care about that particular skill. In fact, the first time the quarterback throws the

Do they want all of you? Or just part of you?

ball, the coach says, "Hey, we don't throw the ball. What are you trying to do?"

It doesn't matter how good the quarterback is; his ability is not going to be reflected in what he is asked to do by this coach. As long as he remains on the team, he'll feel inadequate. And, worse, he'll be regarded as a failure because in the end, what he's really good at isn't needed or valued.

The quarterback has to ask himself, "How much of my capacity, my strengths, and my abilities are being used by this team?" Everyone's level is different, depending on how high a priority they put on their own happiness. For me, it's about 80 percent because I need to spend some of my time running the business instead of coaching. What's your priority on your happiness?

Like the quarterback, you have tremendous skills to offer. And you may have presented a whole list of what you could do for an employer or a client. But if that company only needs 20 percent, in most cases they'll take what they need and overlook the rest. They're not looking at your capacity—they are looking at what they think they need right now. In fact, it's quite possible they just hired you to do one thing for them, such as fix a single problem Most companies have no appreciation for the fact that their top performers may be underutilized. That is, they've hired a five-thousand-yard passing quarterback, but they've put them on a running play team.

Remember my friend, the high-powered derivatives player who was stuck in a bank where they expected him to be a high-priced minder? After a few frustrating months on the job, he called me and we worked together to help him address the elephant in the room. He was in a "wrong fit" job.

"How am I going to deal with this?" he asked me.

"You have to face up to your boss," I replied.

After nine months, my friend finally approached his boss about leaving. The initial response was, "Have you lost your mind?" The job came with a seven-figure income, prestige, and even further opportunity to advance.

But the derivatives player had the courage to say, "You guys aren't going to use me properly. And I'm not doing anything except sitting in my office reading reports and going to meetings. I can't recall the last time I made a decision."

Now he's running his own money management business: "I'm a business builder, not a business maintainer. I could feel the inner turmoil that came from not doing what I thought I should be doing. I compare it to now. I make considerably less money and I work my tail off for fourteen hours a day. But now I feel so much less stress and am so much happier.

"The insights about who you are may seem obvious afterwards," he said. "But you don't come to the conclusions on your own until you think about them in a particular framework.... It is not always easy to figure out what we really want. There are other elements that confuse us, like perhaps you have a need for a high profile that could supersede everything else, or an economic need, or you keep a scorecard to make sure you make more money than anyone else."

Sometimes companies need a little nudge to see that an executive is a true fit. One of my friends is the best disaster recovery businessman I have ever met. His unorthodox approach and willingness to do things that others won't is remarkable. After leaving a very high-profile job as a CEO in which he had performed miracles on a business that was going over a cliff, he was wondering what was next. Shortly thereafter, another friend approached me.

"You know Bob better than anyone," he said. "Can you give me the good and the bad on him? We are thinking of bringing him in."

My response was, "No, I won't, but I will tell you that Bob is the best at saving and building businesses. If you bring him in, you need to give him carte blanche to get full value out of him."

"Nobody gets carte blanche," he replied.

"Then don't hire him," I said. "It won't work."

They hired him, they gave him carte blanche, and so far he's done another outstanding job. They understood that they needed him, and they wanted both his skills and style. It was a true fit.

Capacity utilization is a key consideration for entrepreneurs too. I was in a discussion with a global search firm about possibly joining them. The partners were intrigued by my company's unique way of recruiting. I thought the firm understood that my approach to the business was different from theirs. I thought they were interested in my way of doing business. So imagine my surprise when someone from the company in an interview informed me, "While we're excited about having you, you know that you're not going to be able to do all the things you now do with your particular approach at our firm."

My view was that I could help them be more like my firm. But instead of trying to use me as a role model and consider how I could be used to train others, they were trying to dismantle me. "You're looking to utilize only this much of my capacity," I said. "Thanks. But no thanks. Don't try to fit me into your box."

If I'd allowed my business to become part of that global firm, I would only have been able to use part of what I'm really good at for them. If they didn't want me to do what I do best, then I didn't want any part of them. They were looking at me the wrong way. If someone is interested in buying your company, or bringing you in as a partner, ask yourself if they are looking at you in the right way.

IT'S UP TO YOU

It is your responsibility to make it clear that you want clients that use your capacity to the fullest.

An interior designer I know completed a closet makeover for a client as a favour. But from then on, she kept getting referrals from the client for other closet projects. "I like the money," she said. "But I am so much more than a closet designer. In fact, if I get too many closet projects, I won't have time to do the larger, more challenging space design projects that I love and am good at doing." Finally the designer met with the client and presented an overview of the kind of work she prefers. Within weeks, she received two more, appropriate referrals—and not a single closet makeover.

When you start looking at a potential job through the lens of capacity utilization, it becomes clear pretty quickly whether the job is a true fit or not. One banking executive I advised, for instance, is really good at building strategies that can actually be implemented. When he started working with me, he wrote down his great strengths, which are formulating strategy and making it actionable, working well with clients, and being respected by employees. Then he was recruited by an independent global financial services firm.

Having been invited to dinner with the CEO, the executive put his infomercial into action. Over drinks, he said what the company would get when they hired him. He explained what he would bring to the job, his style of working, and the way in which he would build the business.

"I need to explain how I feel this business should be run," he told his prospective boss. "If you hire me, then this is how I'm going to do it. So hopefully you're going to agree with me and I'll consider the offer, or we're just going to have a nice dinner and then go our separate ways."

Then he asked the key questions: Does this position maximize my utilization of things I'm good at? Are there more people here that I work best with and do they resolve conflict in a similar or compatible fashion? Do I get to do every day the things that I want to do? The answer to each of these questions was yes, so he ended up in a job that's a true fit for him.

These three questions can help you assess whether an opportunity—be it a job or a business opportunity or a new client—is a true fit for you. In an interview, when both sides realize that there's a true fit, the heads around the table start moving up and down like those bobbing-head dogs in the rear windows of cars. That's when someone knows that their message has resonated. But if at some point during an interview they hear the words "But we don't need that," that's okay; they're done. As Jane discovered, it gives you the confidence to say no.

In fact, "no" is good. If you end up being hired for the wrong job, you'll be judged on what you don't do best. It will eventually lead to failure, and you'll wear it. You want to say no to that job.

"No" is good.

And if the hiring committee still insists on going back to its checklist of those standard interview questions, such as "Tell us about a time when you had to collaborate on a team," then it might be time to end the interview. They obviously didn't hear what you just said. Or if they stare at you like those faces on Mount Rushmore, it's pretty clear they don't get what you're telling them.

"No" is good. It gives you a chance to say yes to a job that is a true fit. Then you'll be judged on what you do best.

THAT FIRST JOB

It works, even if you're shooting for your first big job after college. After graduating from the University of Toronto's Rotman School of Management, Ali talked to career coaches. They all wanted her to focus on what the employer wanted. She had a CV that listed her academic achievements and summer jobs. "Basically, it had a lot of words that didn't mean anything," she said.

Naturally, she was just focused on getting a job. "People just think, 'If I get this job, I'll take it' and won't think twice about whether it is right for me," she said afterwards. "So you go into an interview thinking you're just going to make up a version of yourself that you think they want to hear."

It was stressful. So Ali came to me. Right away she realized the problem: "I didn't know how to properly articulate my value and my strengths to a prospective employer. I had to figure out my strengths and how to convey those strengths to an interviewer."

We worked on the four questions to develop her infomercial. She gained a lot of confidence in the process. "Instead of feeling 'If this doesn't work out, my life is over,' it made me ask, 'Is this what I really want to do; is it really what fits well with *me?*'"

The next interview was different. "It was less about portraying myself in a certain way and more about just being honest. As a result, there was energy in the air and it felt more like a discussion than questions being fired at me."

Ali got the job. She learned from the experience the importance of giving the interviewing team a clear picture of who she is and why they should hire her, as well as using the infomercial to determine if the job was going to be a right fit for her.

When you've been in school all your life, it is difficult to think of your identity as anything other than a student. But at the beginning of a whole new stage of life you have the rare luxury of starting fresh, of making a choice. You'll be much farther ahead in the future if you take the time now to do an infomercial and figure out what you really want to do beyond just a job title. Who am I? Have I liked being around other students, or have I spent a lot of my time on my own? What has come easily to me in my studies? What have I struggled with?

As I tell students, a true fit isn't about getting the job; it's about getting the right job. You need to hold on and know that eventually the right opportunity is going to show up.

It's true that young people straight out of college may only have a handful of summer jobs as work experience. But the infomercial still works for them as a way to define what they're good at and who they want to work with. They can still vet job opportunities through the lens of the three concepts—target-rich environment, personality bandwidth, and capacity utilization.

Once you are prepared with an infomercial, there are a few principles of networking you need to follow:

- *Research the hiring company*
  I'm amazed at the number of people who come for an interview who haven't done any research on the hiring company.

When asked "Do you want to know anything more about our organization?" they actually say "No"!

- *Dress for the job*
  Personal presentation matters. Consider the appropriate attire for the industry you're applying to and dress accordingly.
- *Remember those who help you*
  I've placed people in great jobs. They say they really appreciate it, and promise that when it's time to hire, they'll send business my way, but they don't. Then they lose that great job. Who do you think they phone first for help? It's a lesson. Remember the people who help you on the way up. Then you can turn to them if you get into trouble.
- *Educate, don't sell*
  Whether you are networking or going for a job interview, educate, don't sell. The clearer the people you are talking with are about who you are, the more

likely the result is going to be the right one, whether the answer is yes or no. Let people see you through your own eyes; put yourself into the role and educate them about how you would go about executing the job.

chapter 6

STAY TRUE TO YOU

Growth is painful. Change is painful. But nothing is as painful as staying stuck somewhere you don't belong.

—Mandy Hale

Before we go any further, let's talk about temptation. You are going to be tempted to stray from your infomercial when a job comes along that's partly right for you. Maybe it uses some of your skills but not all of them. Maybe the people in the organization are not exactly the kind you like to work with. But the job sounds good. It pays well. It comes with a nice title.

This is when you'll be tempted to shelve your infomercial. Don't. You can't make it right. It will only be a partial fit. How happy do you think you'll be?

Most people consider a job or an opportunity for all sorts of reasons, most of them wrong: it's a promotion, which comes with more money, more prestige, or both. Some might be swayed by simple things. A feeling of "I deserve it," of "It's my turn," of "I've been here a long time" or "I'm better than the person who's currently doing it." I've even known individuals who would rather get picked for the wrong job, just to have the option of turning it down.

Thoughts like these can easily pull people away from their true fit. The job looks good, so they grab it, if only to make sure the person next door doesn't get it and move ahead. Don't get me wrong. There's nothing wrong with pouncing on an opportunity. But it has got to be a *true fit*. Otherwise, you're headed for a disaster that will waste your time and undermine your brand in the process.

Why do people find it so hard to resist the urge to compete for the wrong job? I think it's because they're afraid to stand up for themselves—for who they really are. I see this in my coaching practice almost every day. They are afraid that if they are themselves, and if they say who they are, they will miss opportunities. And they think that if they miss opportunities, they won't get any more. No more jobs, no more clients, no more business offers.

That's the fear I sense lurking under the surface when I ask my clients why they felt the need to take the wrong job or pick the wrong client. Does it make sense? Of course not! These people are successful. But they're still scared they'll miss the boat unless they say yes. That's why they are willing to try to turn themselves into someone else.

Last spring, for example, I got a call from one of my friends, a book publisher, who was skiing at Whistler. She sounded anxious.

"Jim, I've got a really bad feeling," she said.

"What's wrong?"

"I've just read the contract one of my authors sent me. It says that my designer, editor, and writer have to file time sheets and account for every six minutes of their time on the job."

"That's not a client for you," I said.

"I know, but it's a high-profile job, with some of the biggest stars in the music business. It could be a real coup for us. So why do I feel so miserable?"

"Because it's not a good fit for you," I said. "That's not who you are. You want clients who value what you do and how you do it."

That morning, the publisher wrote a brief note to the author to say she was pulling out of the deal because it was not a good fit. "I felt so light, so happy, when I was skiing that day," she later told me.

So why would the publisher even consider working with someone who's a micromanager? It's hard to say no to the money and the status of the job, but that's what she had to do. After sending the note to the client, she mulled over her decision, wondering if she'd find any other authors to fill the gap. But several weeks later, after returning to Toronto, she called to say she had landed two great clients.

As I told the publisher, it's okay to be you. It is okay to say this is who I am, this is what I'm good it, these are the people I get along with, and this is what I want to do every day for the rest of my life. And like my publisher friend discovered, it's going to be okay when you say no. You have to be prepared to walk away from the big client, the senior position, the money in order to stay true to you.

Take Emma, a budding young Toronto chef. Emma provided her client with a per-person estimate for a dinner party based on the kind of event and service required. Her client clearly wanted Emma's skills but wanted to negotiate the price in order to lower it. "What if I bought the fish?" she asked. "And could we save money on servers if I asked my nanny and housekeeper to help out?"

Emma was forced to step back and think about this. Her personal brand was clearly at stake. The dinner party guests wouldn't know that her client had bought the fish or used inexperienced servers. (It's not as if she could put a sign by the fish saying "My client bought this, not me.")

The accountability all fell to Emma. She had to say, "Sorry, that won't work for me. There may be other chefs out there that would work better for what you want to do, but that's not how I go about my business. I either quote you a price or work from a price that you would like to spend. I control all aspects of the event from start to finish. That way I can manage the quality control to my standards." Needless to say she—fortunately—did not get the job. Nice miss, Emma!

Going forward, Emma knew she needed to either provide a price and stick with it or ask for a budget and set up the menu and service accordingly. Anything outside of that format would diminish her personal brand. A week later, she landed another event where she was in charge, soup to nuts.

Emma used her infomercial to stay true to who she was—not just someone with the title "chef"—and to keep doing what she's really good at. It also helped her identify those she needed to "fire" as clients, particularly when someone was trying to dismantle her. And it helped her to stay true to her pricing rather than let someone else define her value. In marketing talk, this is clearly what is known as managing and protecting her brand. And guess what? In 2015, she won the Chopped Canada contest.

I know it's scary, but you'll find it feels great to stick to your true fit when a prospect wants to chip away at it. One time, I explained to a prospective client that my fees were based on 25 percent of the first-year compensation. "Are you negotiable?" he asked. After a long pause, I responded, "Normally not, but if you want to pay me 30 percent, then I'm open to it." The prospect was taken aback. No, he said, he meant the price would go lower. By then, I knew he wasn't the right client for me. If the most important factor to him was price, we would never get along well. That's not the kind of people I want to work with. They will never appreciate or value my service accordingly, so why would I work with them?

That's protecting your brand. And it's just another example of how to stay true to you. The more you stay true to you, the more you'll attract the right people, the more others will see you as someone they both want and need, and the happier you'll be.

chapter 7

GETTING OUT OF A WRONG FIT

Your value does not decrease based on someone's inability to see your worth.

—Hindi proverb

When I was growing up, no one would have dared utter the words "I want to be happy in my job." I can only imagine the scornful response from parents and teachers: "What are you talking about? A job's a job's a job. Shut up and do your homework."

I want to be happy in my job.

That was then. We were not expected to be happy at work. We just went out and got a job. These days, you can make a choice. Do you want to be happy at work? Or do you want to settle for a job that's "good enough," even though it's not a good fit for you?

If you are unhappy at work, there's a natural tendency to complain about your job and do nothing about it. If this is the case, you aren't willing to do what it takes to change the situation. And that's okay. But if you decide to do nothing, at least stop banging your head against the wall. Stop moaning about your job. And be aware that staying in a job you dislike, or working around people who constantly make you feel uncomfortable, can make your work suffer. You can waste years of your life not realizing the reputational damage that you're doing to yourself on a daily basis. It just chips away until everyone can see that you're totally disengaged.

THE POWER TO CHOOSE

You don't have to live and work like that, though. You have the power to make a choice, and an infomercial can help. By looking at what's revealed in your infomercial—what do you genuinely love to do, for instance, and how much of your capacity is being used—you'll be forced to look in the mirror and come to terms with where you are at in your working life. Then you can choose to stay or to go.

Martha, for instance, graduated from university and found a job managing a small retail store. She needed the money and figured it was entry-level experience. But she soon found herself stuck in a job where there was no opportunity for movement, the salary was low, and she wasn't enjoying her work.

One day her boss decided to give her hourly rate a modest boost. He needed sales help and hoped it would encourage her to remain a bit longer. "I'm glad to have a raise," she told the manager. "But I don't see myself staying on the sales side. It isn't what I enjoy the most and it doesn't use what I think I'm really good at doing."

Martha then pulled out a written page with a list of where she felt her skills could contribute to the business side of the operation: creating a store manual, setting up a proper hiring process, participating in the buying decisions. Her boss was surprised—he had no idea that she was interested in the business beyond a sales job. Turns out, his senior office manager and buyer was leaving, and he was trying to figure out how to fill the vacancy. Martha was the ideal candidate, and shortly afterward she began working in her new position. She stayed, and was happy for it.

If you confront your boss, you should remember that it can sometimes lead to the exit sign. Take Brian, a senior executive in the financial business.

He was a business builder, but after a change in senior management, Brian's new boss didn't want to build business; in fact, he preferred to shrink it. Everything Brian was good at wasn't needed by his new boss. But he didn't want to quit because he'd be giving up a juicy severance package, plus other monies owed. When we worked together, I told Brian: "You have to be true to yourself, and push your boss to keep growing the business. He'll either say you're right, and let you do what you're good at, or he'll get tired of it and fire you—either way, you are a winner. But the status quo won't work because you'll continue to be unhappy and underutilized."

Brian became a "respectful irritant." Every time he met with his boss, he kept pushing for growth plans, and each time, his ideas were turned down. As his boss's patience grew thin, Brian eventually was able to say to him, "I'm a growth guy. I build business. Either you let me do what I was hired to do, or you exit me." He got fired but with a severance package.

Brian found a way to stay true to himself. By using his infomercial, he could state clearly why he was hired and then use the conversation to force a choice with his boss. He never felt better.

It's not always possible to take action, as Brian and Martha did, to fix a miserable situation at work. I often see executives who are unhappy at work after they've been brought in from another company. Big corporations, for example, are notorious for making it difficult for external candidates to enter at the senior levels. They're heavily dominated by long-standing employees, and when someone comes in from the outside, they can smell whether or not that person has been given power and air support. If not, there's absolutely nothing in it for the long-time employees to help that person survive. So the new hire just disappears into the quagmire, frustrated and definitely not happy.

George, for instance, has seen first-hand what happens when external candidates are brought in at the senior level of large, complex institutions. At one point in his career, George was very interested in a senior position at a corporation. Following a successful meeting with the CEO, who could see the kind of business improvements George would bring, the CEO suggested George meet with the next line level of partners. "When those people found out I was coming in to see them, they wanted no part of it," George recalled. "It wasn't personal. They just didn't want anyone else who'd been more successful or more senior coming in. I knew then that it just wasn't going to work."

YOU'RE FIRED!

Getting fired rarely comes as a surprise to the people who come to see me. The institution either didn't need them anymore or didn't want them. In other words, they might have needed their skills but didn't want them—just the way they do business. Sometimes it's the other way round: the person fit in just fine, but the organization didn't need the skills that person could offer. And most figure that out by the time the end comes.

There are lots of ways to lose a job. You can be shown the door because of a merger, a sell-off, or a downsizing exercise. Whatever the reason, you have to come to terms with what happened and be able to talk about it without extreme emotion.

The process can leave you feeling completely at loose ends. Without a familiar title or position—the CEO, president, director—you feel you've lost your identity. As one man put it after leaving a high-profile position: "The biggest challenge for me after leaving my job was to get to know myself again. I had just been doing work for so long, keeping my head down for so long, I had kind of forgotten who I was."

The situation is similar when elected representatives leave public life. As one Canadian politician put it: "After many years in office, I had to rediscover myself again because after doing such an all-consuming job, I had become 'the job.' Even though I knew one day it would come to an end, when it was over, I had to ask, 'Who the hell am I?'" He did the "true fit" work: he wrote his infomercial and eventually re-established himself in a new career as a teacher, public speaker, and author.

The first time I sit down with someone recently fired, I explain how their career has unfolded up until now. Typically, they've moved ahead by jumping at opportunities that present themselves along the way. They haven't taken the time to ask themselves what they're actually good at, and what they like to do. I tell them that even though it's tough to get fired, it opens up a great opportunity. Losing a job makes them desperate enough to sit down and write their own infomercial. It means they can finally find out who they really are—and finally make a clear choice about the job that's a true fit for them. It marks the day they can look forward to doing what they love to do.

Take my client Kate, who had just been fired. We both knew that her having been fired from her previous job would be the elephant in the room in any interview. So before she could see anyone, she needed to be able to articulate—quickly, and without emotion—why she was let go.

No one presents well at this early stage. Kate practised her "leaving story" in front of a video camera as an exercise at an outplacement firm. She was shocked when the video was played back to her. She thought she had been telling her story well, but the playback showed her face twitching every time she mentioned the subject. After several weeks of intensive counselling, the video was shot again. This time Kate passed with flying colours.

No twitching, blinking, squirming, or emotion: just a calm, short explanation before she moved on to the next topic.

Next, Kate needed to find someone who needed her and wanted her. No one would know whether they did until they had better insight into who she was, through her infomercial. The answers leading to her infomercial forced her to drill down to who she was—totally apart from the role she once was given or the title she held. It gave her the assurance that she'd move into something that was a true fit for her agenda—for what she liked to do—not someone else's.

Although the emotional toll and financial costs of getting fired can be high, when someone like Kate is, as we say, "given a chance to pursue new opportunities," it can turn out to be the best thing that could have happened. Kate, for instance, subsequently founded her own communications business and became the author of several books. And she's not alone.

There are dozens of stories of individuals who were fired at least once before they found a career that was a true fit: J.K. Rowling, Jerry Seinfeld, Lee

Iacocca, even Walt Disney (apparently he "lacked imagination and had no good ideas"). Thomas Edison took on inventing full-time after he got fired from Western Union. Early in his career, the distracted inventor spilled some battery acid, which then ate through the floor and landed on his boss's desk. In 1985, Steve Jobs was fired by Apple—the very company he had founded. John Sculley, who ousted Jobs, admitted recently that removing Jobs had been a mistake on the part of Apple. And many years after the firing, Jobs noted, "I didn't see it then, but it turned out that getting fired from Apple was the best thing that could have ever happened to me."

"I WAS LUCKY TO GET MY FOOT IN THE DOOR"

Clearly, losing your job can be a real challenge, but so can beginning a job. Particularly if you are just starting a career, things can go off track very quickly, especially if you took the first job you found.

I can always tell when I ask, "So how's it going?" They say, "Great. Well… not quite what I expected... but then, it is a job," or "I've been very lucky to get my foot in the door; not sure it's the right door" [laughs uncomfortably], or the classic, "I need to give it time, but the money's good."

I don't try to convince them to leave a job. I just help them realize there are other opportunities out there, if they're willing to do the work to find the true fit.

WHAT DO YOU DO IF YOU'RE UNHAPPY AT WORK?

Step 1: Assess your situation.

- Is your capacity being used to the full?
- Do your personality and conflict-resolution style fit in with those of your colleagues?
- Is your job your idea of the perfect day?

Step 2: Sit down with your supervisor. Explain what you are good at doing, what you enjoy doing, and who you work best with. Then ask if there are other opportunities in the organization that would be a better fit for you.

If you get a positive answer, good for you. You've taken responsibility and made a change for the better. You should be closer to what you have defined as your perfect day.

If you get a negative answer, you should either

- acknowledge your lot, decide to stay, and stop moaning about it, or
- quit and look for another job.

Answering these three questions helps you recognize the reality of where you are; going through the process gives you the information you need to decide whether to stay or to go.

chapter 8

YES ... BUT

I'm a big fan of people being exactly who they are.

***—Kelly Foster (Scarlett Johansson) in the film* We Bought a Zoo**

I know that the True Fit process is possible from my professional experience, as a manager who has hired hundreds of people, and as a coach of many individuals across diverse industries. And these are not just stories of a career that's successful in terms of a position or money. People tell me that working through the four core questions from Chapter 4 and the three key concepts in Chapter 5 made them believe in themselves again and gave them a reason to get up in the morning.

And yet I do sometimes hear objections, like these:

YES ... BUT IT SOUNDS TOO EASY

The objection I hear most often is: "What you're talking about is for dreamers." True, on the surface, the questions seem simple. But the process is hard, very hard. The issue of wrong fit in corporations and the misery people face every day in their jobs can't be solved just by going through a few questions. Digging down takes time and courage, especially when you've spent most of your life not knowing who you are or what you want. It's worth it, says this former politician: "Humans tend not to have self-awareness built into their psyches. We are much less self-aware than we think we are.... By knowing yourself, your strengths and weaknesses, you emerge in the end much stronger, with more confidence and a better understanding of what you like and what you want to do."

YES ... BUT I JUST NEED TO WIN THE INTERVIEW TO GET THE JOB

An interview is never about winning the job or winning over the interviewer. It's a conversation to see whether you can see yourself fitting into a particular work environment and whether the hiring committee understands what they will get if they hire you. If they don't need or want you, that's great. You both can walk away. Imagine what would have happened if they'd hired you!

YES ... BUT WHAT IF I'M OFFERED A JOB THAT USES PART OF WHAT I REALLY ENJOY DOING?

Often things get off track during the job interview when you get your chance to say, "Here are the three things I'm really good at" and the interviewer replies to the effect of "Well, I'm not interested in one, or two, or three, but this little part over here, I can use a bit of that." And because you want the job, you give in.

Don't let this happen. Don't let anyone sell you into a job—and don't sell yourself into a job.

You should be able to clearly articulate what an employer should pay you for. And you should be looking for someone who says, "I need all of it, not just 20 percent!" If this is not the case, walk away.

YES ... BUT I'M ON THEIR SUCCESSION PLAN!

You're smart. Maybe you were at the top of your class in school. Or you've been recruited to a position because the company is in awe of where you worked before or what they've heard you accomplished. And now you're trapped because you realize it is a wrong fit, but the company is trying to woo you with all sorts of promises if you stay. But do you even want to move up? Listen to what my friend the derivatives player told me: "They thought that moving up in the hierarchy in the company was going to be something that made me happy. But when I took a good look at what mattered to me, hierarchy was irrelevant. It was low down on the list of things I consider to be rewarding."

If you do want to move up, ask yourself, Are you really on the succession plan? Most likely not. Instead, you'll probably spend only a small part of your time doing what you are really good at doing, and your dissatisfaction and frustration will grow. You won't feel valued because you are not excelling where your skills are strong. Your performance will suffer, you will become disengaged. It is at this point, typically, that your boss will say, "Let's get rid of her," not "Let's find the right fit for her."

YES ... BUT THE MONEY IS GOOD

Measuring success and personal value goes far beyond monetary aspects. I've never been happier with the work I do now, despite the fact that I make significantly less money than in my previous careers. And I'm not alone; I hear this from people all the time.

"I had one of the top twenty jobs in the country," said my friend in derivatives. "I made a seven-figure income. I liked the people I was working with, and the job came with lots of prestige. But I still walked away from it. Every day I could feel the stress in my stomach, sitting in my office not doing what I thought I should be doing. I was a Tasmanian devil, and the institution where I worked just didn't want that much disturbance."

Research is clear about one thing: we all get better at the things we enjoy doing, our productivity jumps by leaps and bounds, our expertise increases, and, above all, we're happier.

The same principle applies to our work life.

YES ... BUT I CAN CHANGE—I CAN LEARN TO DO THAT

Your life should be focused on working every day on your strengths. You should find a job or career that requires as little as possible from that side of your balance sheet where you've listed "things I suck at."

When you lack strengths in one area, why would you spend your time trying to improve your weakness when you could improve what you're really good at doing? Instead of promising to change, get others to see you through the right lens and say, "Here's why you should be interested in me. Here's what you should not try to change."

Steve, the guy who walked into a food fight in his new job, put it this way: "People tend to look at their weaknesses, want to take a course, and get more information on things they're not so good at. In the limited time you have in your working career, I learned you really need to focus on things you are really good at doing."

YES ... BUT IN MY POSITION I CAN'T AFFORD TO BE THAT FUSSY

New graduates often tell me that they just need to get their foot in the door somewhere. I say back to them, "Shouldn't it be the right door?" Of course you can afford to be fussy. We all deserve to be fussy when it comes to our working lives. Falling into a career just because you got hired somewhere shouldn't be the basis for how you spend the rest of your working life.

YES ... BUT IT SOUNDS LIKE A LOT OF WORK

I am not denying that it is a lot of work. And it's difficult. It can take time to put together an infomercial, define your target-rich environment, figure out your conflict-resolution style, and assess just how much capacity you need to use in order to be happy at your job. It's also tough to sit down with a boss and say you don't have the personality bandwidth to do sales, even though the job represents a promotion. It's even more difficult to turn down a job offer when you know they may need your skills, but they do not want you or the way you work.

But for those who've gone through the process, it's worth it. If it leads to a no, or a change of careers, you've been spared from a job where you'll eventually be miserable. And if it leads to a yes, you'll have what most people only dream about—a job you love every hour of the day, doing exactly what you like to do.

Here's what one of my clients said: "I came out with a higher level of self awareness. This is who I am and this is what I'm good at. It was an empowering experience. I know who I am, and what I'm really, really good at doing. And because I've now accepted this, my business is a success, and every day I spend at work is as close to my perfect day as I ever imagined it could be."

CONCLUSION: A TRUE FIT IS UP TO YOU

**Be real, be yourself,
be unique, be true, be honest,
be humble, be happy.**

I can't tell you what to do. I can just lead you on the right path. As a behaviourist, I believe you reach the right result through a process of doing the right things. The process is what counts. If you don't follow the process, you might get a good result, but you really won't know what it will be. As I like to say, if you don't know where you're going, any bus will get you there.

The choice is always up to you.

The power is always in your hands to prepare yourself properly and, if you want, to make a change. This will happen if you follow the process I've described in *True Fit*. It will give you and those who meet you a clear picture of who you are. I hope it will give you the confidence to be you.

Knowing who you are is empowering. You know now that if you live each day with all four categories in your "infomercial" fulfilled, you've got a home run. But you have to stick to it. If even one of the four categories in your infomercial does not match your current situation, then you're in a wrong fit. If that job isn't using all of your capabilities, you're in a wrong fit. If you're not compatible with those around you, you're not going to be successful. It doesn't matter how good you are. If most of the people around you resolve conflict in an avoidance manner, and you're competitive, you'll just spend your time browbeating everyone.

The change won't happen immediately, but over time, if you stick to a true fit, you'll see better opportunities, and more people will direct the right opportunities your way

I can't say that you'll get a job that pays $10 million, or that you'll rise to CEO, or even keep your job. But if you have an infomercial that accurately reflects who you are, it will lead you to finding the true fit for you.

It can even help you be a better manager and change the lives of the people who work for you. I've seen this happen with one of my own clients. John is the director of a mergers and acquisitions (M&A) division at a financial services company. After twenty-five years in the business, he finds that most graduates automatically look to land jobs in either investment banking or consulting, even though these positions might not be a good fit for them. "They get this idea in their head," he said, "even though it isn't something they should necessarily be doing. In fact, some definitely are not going to be good in either of these areas, but everyone wants go in this direction because everyone else is doing it."

John was worried about one of his employees. There was no doubt that the woman, who was in her twenties, understood the financial markets, but she was not as strong in terms of analytics and modelling capabilities as others on her team. Although she was willing to try to improve, something which John admired, he felt there were other places in the company where she'd be more successful—and happier.

"She was very good from a communications and marketing standpoint," he explained. "I felt that instead of being the average or below-average performer where she was, she could move to be above average, even a superstar, in a different division. Leveraging her strengths might actually lead her to be in a better place, with a higher chance of success and happiness."

It was a good call. The employee was transferred to a job that was a better fit for her, and John made sure that new hires came in with top skills in analytics, which is what he really needed.

True Fit can change life not only for you but also for the people around you.

For those who place a high priority on personal happiness and are willing to do something about achieving it, the journey is worth it. I know because I was one of those people. I can't stop from saying what I think. I can't stop being me. And because of that, I'm happier, healthier, and more productive than I've ever been in my life. You can be too.

SAMPLE INFOMERCIAL

Jim Beqaj

Trusted Advisor
Human Capital

What I am good at

- I have hired over 600 people during my career
- I was the chief architect and executer for the building of numerous businesses, such as derivatives and high-yield, globally
- I have coached and mentored many people throughout my career

People I work best with

- People who can trust me and delegate responsibility to me
- People who need someone to determine or help with strategy and then execute that strategy
- People who are truly open to a different approach
- People who are not micromanagers

Conflict Resolution

- I am collaborative in my efforts to seek the right answer
- I am open to compromise when the right answer, for whatever reason, can't be executed

Perfect Day

- Pitching and working on recruiting, consulting, and coaching assignments
- Interacting with clients in above three categories

REFERENCES

Adkins, Amy. "Majority of U.S. Employees Not Engaged Despite Gains in 2014." *gallup.com*, January 28, 2015. Retrieved from http://www.gallup.com/poll/181289/majority-employees-not-engaged-despite-gains-2014.aspx.

Bateson, John, Jochen Wirtz, Eugene Burke, and Carly Vaughan. "When Hiring, First Test, and Then Interview." *Harvard Business Review*, November 2013. Retrieved from https://hbr.org/2013/11/when-hiring-first-test-and-then-interview.

Bort, Julie. "John Sculley: Steve Jobs 'was never fired' from Apple." *businessinsider.com*, May 21, 2015. Retrieved from http://www.businessinsider.com/john-sculley-steve-jobs-was-never-fired-from-apple-2015-5.

Canadian Press. "Anthopoulos says staying with Blue Jays not the 'right fit.'" *sportsnet.ca*, October 29, 2015. Retrieved from http://www.sportsnet.ca/baseball/mlb/

anthopoulos-says-staying-with-blue-jays-not-the-right-fit/.

CBS News. "Study: Most Americans unhappy at work." *cbsnews.com*, June 25, 2013. Retrieved http://www.cbsnews.com/news/study-most-americans-unhappy-at-work/.

Chiose, Simona. "Documents show UBC board had issues with president's leadership style." *The Globe and Mail*, January 27, 2016. Retrieved from http://www.theglobeandmail.com/news/national/education/ubc-letters-reveal-tense-relations-with-former-president/article28411696/.

Christian-Taylor, Kema. "5 Warning Signs That Mean You Shouldn't Take The Job." *forbes.com*, April 11, 2016. Retrieved from http://www.forbes.com/sites/kemachristiantaylor/2016/04/11/5-warning-signs-that-mean-you-shouldnt-take-the-job/#379a887a2757.

CNW. "Half of Canada's working population is unhappy, Hays Canada study shows." *newswire.ca*, May 2, 2016. Retrieved from http://www.newswire.ca/news-releases/

half-of-canadas-working-population-is-unhappy-hays-canada-study-shows-577775571.html.

Edwards, Jim. "Former Apple CEO John Sculley admits Steve Jobs never forgave him, and he never repaired their friendship, before Jobs died." *uk.businessinsider.com*, May 27, 2015. Retrieved from http://uk.businessinsider.com/john-sculley-admits-steve-jobs-never-forgave-him-before-jobs-died-2015-5.

HR Morning. "Why the interview process is flawed." *hrmorning.com*, January 24, 2014. Retrieved from http://www.hrmorning.com/why-the-interview-process-is-flawed/.

Kahney, Leander. "John Sculley On Steve Jobs, The Full Interview Transcript." *cultofmac.com*, October 14, 2010. Retrieved from http://www.cultofmac.com/63295/john-sculley-on-steve-jobs-the-full-interview-transcript/.

Macleod, Robert. "After rocky start, Mark Shapiro steers Blue Jays with help from Paul Beeston." *The Globe and Mail*, January 15, 2016. Retrieved from http://www.theglobeandmail.com/sports/baseball/

after-rocky-start-mark-shapiro-steers-blue-jays-with-help-from-paul-beeston/article28229732/.

Mindflash. "Infographic: How Much A Bad Hire Will Actually Cost You." *fastcompany.com*, April 18, 2014. Retrieved from http://www.fastcompany.com/3028628/work-smart/infographic-how-much-a-bad-hire-will-actually-cost-you/1.

Rouen, Ethan. "Is it better to hire for cultural fit over experience?" *fortune.com*, April 28, 2011. Retrieved from http://fortune.com/2011/04/28/is-it-better-to-hire-for-cultural-fit-over-experience/.

Schofield, Kerry. "Cultural Fit In The Workplace: How Personality Affects Hiring And Teamwork." *eremedia.com*, June 21, 2013. Retrieved from http://www.eremedia.com/ere/cultural-fit-in-the-workplace-how-personality-affects-hiring-and-teamwork/.

INDEX

ABOUT THE AUTHOR

As former president of Wood Gundy, Jim Beqaj has personally hired over 600 people in his business career. Among other achievements, he led the integration of Wood Gundy with CIBC, and its expansion into the U.S. in the early 1990s. Since 2002, Jim has been a coach and adviser, helping corporate clients attract talented teams and individuals who fit each business and culture.

Jim also co-founded BayStreetDirect.com, an online IPO and private placement company that revolutionized the way securities were delivered to the public. In 2000, it was ranked 11 out of the top 25 internet companies.

Beqaj lives in Toronto with his wife, Jennifer, and six children.